POP corn!

60 IRRESISTIBLE RECIPES FOR EVERYONE'S FAVORITE SNACK

TEXT AND RECIPES BY
FRANCES TOWNER GIEDT

DESIGN AND ILLUSTRATIONS BY
BARBARA BALCH

SIMON & SCHUSTER

NEW YORK   LONDON   TORONTO   SYDNEY   TOKYO   SINGAPORE

**SIMON &
SCHUSTER**

Rockefeller Center
1230 Avenue of the Americas
New York, NY 10020

Popcorn! was conceived and produced by Miller and O'Shea, Inc.
3 Stony Point Road
Westport, CT 06880

Manufactured in the United States of America

10 9 8 7 6 5 4 3 2

Library of Congress Cataloging-in-Publication Data

Giedt, Frances Towner.
    Popcorn! / text and recipes by Frances Towner Giedt : design and illustration by Barbara Balch.
        p. cm.
    1. Cookery (Popcorn) 2. Popcorn. I. Title.
  TX814.5.P66G54 1995   95–23951
  641.6'5677—dc20   CIP

ISBN: 0-684-81190-1

Contents

Savory Popcorn Concoctions

Sweet Popcorn Confections

Banana Praline, 39

Better-Than-Jack 40

Butterscotch Toffee, 42

California Combo, 44

Caramel Fudge, 45

Caramel Peanut, 46

Chocolate Crunch, 49

Cinnamon, 50

Cranberry, 53

Grape, 54

Honey Almond Crunch, 55

Honey Orange. 58

Key Lime, 59

Macadamia Butter Crunch, 60

Maple Toasted Pecan, 62

Mocha Almond, 63

Peanut Butter Crunch, 64

Pecan Almond Praline, 67

Piña Colada, 68

Pineapple Macadamia, 69

Rocky Road Popcorn Balls, 70

Sassy Lemon, 73

Southern Bourbon Brittle, 74

Spiced Apple, 75

Toasted Cinnamon Corn, Fruit,

and Nut Jumble, 76

Toffee Fudge Crunch, 79

Tutti-Frutti: Cherry, Blueberry,

and Lime, 80

Vanilla Candy Crunch, 81

Skinny Popcorn Combinations

Acknowledgments,

A Bowl of Popped Corn

An all-American favorite, popcorn—the only variety of corn that pops—is hardly a recent discovery. Archaeologists excavating in Peru, Mexico, and the American Southwest have unearthed preserved cobs of popcorn dating back thousands of years. To the early Native Americans, popcorn was a currency of trade and friendship, a symbol of hospitality and fertility. Columbus recorded that natives in the West Indies sold popcorn to his crew.

By the time the colonists arrived on these shores, Native Americans were growing more than 700 varieties of popcorn, although the corn brought to the first Thanksgiving was more likely parched flint corn (the multicolored corn that's often used for decoration), rather than the legendary deerskin bag of popcorn.

Since those early days, we've been sold on popcorn. Every red-blooded moviegoer in America knows the hand-to-mouth motion of popcorn munching. Grown-ups and kids alike hold dear the memory of spending winter evenings in front of a glowing fireplace with a giant bowl of freshly popped corn. Popcorn feeds the soul and calms the nerves—it is undoubtedly the grain of the people.

Now, by popular demand, *Popcorn!* takes that plain movie theater popcorn into the new-age nineties, perhaps even into the millennium.

Eaten plain without any oil or butter, popcorn is a skinny 27 calories per cup. Since it's a whole grain cereal with high fiber content, popcorn has received well-earned recommendations from the American Cancer Society and the National Cancer Institute. It's included on the American Dental Association's list of wholesome sugar-free snacks, and both the American Diabetes Association and the American Dietetic Association allow popcorn as a bread exchange for those on special diets. Gram for gram, popcorn has more protein, phosphorus, iron, and vitamin A than ice cream or crackers.

Nutritionally, air-popped popcorn, made without oil or salt, is the best choice. Otherwise, make the popcorn with a popper which calls for only one teaspoon of oil and make that oil a heart-healthy polyunsaturated or monounsaturated oil such as canola or safflower. Go easy on the salt.

To date, all prepackaged microwave popcorn uses saturated fat and a substantial amount of salt. In the summer of 1994, the Center for Science in the Public Interest shocked movie theatergoers when it revealed that most movie theaters were cooking their popcorn in coconut oil, an oil whose capacity to raise blood cholesterol levels exceeds that of butterfat, beef tallow, and lard. This prompted many movie theater chains to switch to canola oil, which has the lowest saturated fat content of all cooking oils.

Health professionals have been debating the healthfulness of substituting margarine for butter for decades. This dilemma has once again captured public interest with new medical studies that reveal that margarine's trans fatty acids, produced by partially hydrogenating vegetable fat (a process to change liquid vegetable oil to a solid with the texture of butter), are related to high levels of LDL cholesterol and lower levels of HDL cholesterol. They are also suspected to enhance deposits of fat in the arteries and actually interfere with the metabolism of fat. But since butter is a saturated fat, many health professionals advise against cooking with it since it elevates blood cholesterol that can lead to cardiovascular disease. However, butter is a natural product, made without additives. The role of butter or margarine in popcorn is that of adding flavor and helping the seasonings to adhere to the kernels.

If you are on a restricted diet, always follow the advice of your physician or dietitian. In place of butter or margarine, mist the popcorn with butter-flavored vegetable spray or butter-flavored granules that have been reconstituted, according to package directions, before adding the seasonings. Neither the vegetable spray or granules will add any appreciable fat. (See *Skinny Popcorn Combinations*, pp. 84-109, for specific recipes.) Popcorn prepared this way becomes soggy after a few hours. Make the popcorn in small batches and eat it, freshly made, while it's still warm.

For most people, however, until more research on the role of dietary fat in health conclusively ends the butter-versus-margarine controversy, an occasional use of a modest amount of butter or margarine on popcorn, within the framework of a healthy diet, should not pose a medical problem.

An Anytime Snack

Coated with some spices and herbs, popcorn rivals the most expensive off-the-shelf snack food, yet costs just pennies to make. And popcorn is fun to eat. It brings out the kid in all of us—and most of us just can't get enough. As a child, I can remember growing popcorn on our suburban ranch in Kansas. What I remember most is popping the corn in an old metal basket in the fireplace, making popcorn balls for Halloween treats, stringing popcorn for the Christmas tree, and devouring bowls of fluffy white popcorn during study breaks at college.

These recipes give you more reasons to keep on munching—here's a terrific collection of wild, gourmet flavors that you won't find at your local cinema. All recipes start with freshly popped corn made without oil or with a minimum of oil. To get popping, refer to the basic directions for making perfect popcorn below.

Making Basic Popcorn

Popped corn using a hot air popper: Use ¼ cup popcorn for about 2 quarts popped corn; 6 tablespoons popcorn for about 3 quarts popped corn; and ½ cup popcorn for about 4 quarts popped corn. Follow manufacturer's directions.

Popped corn made with oil: Pour 1 tablespoon, or up to ¼ cup, canola or corn oil into a 5- to 6-quart heavy pan over medium-high heat. Once hot (if oil starts to smoke, it's too hot), drop 1 or 2 popcorn kernels into the oil. When the kernel spins or pops, add ½ cup popcorn.

Cover with lid loose enough to allow steam to escape and shake the pan to coat each kernel with the oil. Continue to shake the pan frequently until popping almost stops. Remove from heat. Makes about 4 quarts.

Popped corn using a microwave: If your microwave oven instruction manual recommends popping corn, follow manufacturer's directions using a microwave popper. The yield will be less than popcorn made in a hot air popper or on the stove-top, but the corn can be popped quickly without oil.

Popped corn made on the grill: For each 2-cup serving, place 1 teaspoon oil and 1 tablespoon popcorn on a 16-inch square of heavy-duty aluminum foil. Bring the corner of each square together and twist loosely to seal. Place the packets on a medium-hot grill, about 6 inches from the source of heat. When popping almost stops, remove packets from the grill.

From Spicy to Sweet to Skinny

Once the popcorn's made, simply add some simple, or sophisticated, seasonings to dress it up. For instance, if you like spicy popcorn, there are recipes for Ragin' Cajun, Jalapeño Pecan, Sun-Dried Tomato, Pizza, Sesame Hot Chili, Jamaican Ginger, and Taco.

Anyone with a sweet tooth will easily become addicted to the Butterscotch Toffee, Honey Almond Crunch, Maple Toasted Pecan, and Peanut Butter Crunch. If you're fond of fruit flavors, there are recipes for such delightful concoctions as Banana Praline, Cranberry,

Key Lime, Piña Colada, Sassy Lemon, Spiced Apple, and Tutti-Frutti. Chocoholics will love the Chocolate Crunch, Rocky Road Popcorn Balls, and Toffee Fudge Crunch.

For those on fat-restricted diets, the flavors run the gamut from earthy to spicy to fruity with such blends as Scandinavian Dill, Low-Fat Chocolate, Mexican, Orange, Gingersnap, Cheese and Pepper, or Popcorn and Apple Pie.

There are more than 55 recipes here to excite, delight, and satisfy your urge for popcorn snacking. So start popping, settle back, and dig right in.

Savory Popcorn Concoctions

Easy Mixing

An easy way to mix hot popcorn with butter and seasonings is to put the popcorn in a large paper grocery bag, pour the seasoned butter over the popcorn, close the bag, and shake.

DILL ROMANO

3 tablespoons unsalted butter
½ teaspoon garlic powder
½ teaspoon salt
2 quarts popped corn
2 teaspoons dried dill weed
¼ cup freshly grated Romano cheese

In a small saucepan, melt butter over low heat. Stir in garlic powder and salt. Drizzle butter mixture over popcorn. Sprinkle with dill and Romano cheese. Toss to coat evenly. Store in an airtight container for up to 1 week.

MAKES ABOUT 2 QUARTS

That's a Lot of Popcorn!

According to the Popcorn Institute, Americans consumed more than 18.5 billion quarts of popcorn in 1993—about 73 quarts per man, woman, and child—70 percent of which is eaten in the home.

Popcorn Harvest

In 1900 there were about 20,000 acres of popcorn harvested in the United States. By 1993, this figure had grown to 272,000 acres. Although popcorn is grown in more than 30 states, the major producing states are Illinois, Indiana, Iowa, Kansas, Kentucky, Michigan, Missouri, Nebraska, and Ohio.

EAST INDIAN

¼ cup (½ stick) unsalted butter

1 tablespoon honey

¼ teaspoon cayenne pepper

½ teaspoon garlic powder

½ teaspoon onion powder

½ tablespoon ground cumin

1 teaspoon ground cinnamon

Dash ground allspice

½ teaspoon salt

3 quarts popped corn

Preheat oven to 300° F. Melt butter in a small saucepan over low heat. Add remaining ingredients except popcorn. Cook, stirring, for 1 minute. Pour over popcorn. Toss to coat evenly. Transfer popcorn to a large baking pan. Bake for 5 minutes, stirring twice, until crisped. Store in an airtight container for up to 1 week.

MAKES ABOUT 3 QUARTS

HOT, HOT CURRY

1 tablespoon coriander seeds

1 teaspoon cumin seeds

$\frac{1}{4}$ teaspoon black peppercorns

$\frac{1}{2}$ teaspoon fennel seeds

$\frac{1}{2}$ teaspoon ground turmeric

$\frac{1}{2}$ teaspoon allspice

$\frac{1}{2}$ teaspoon ground mustard

$\frac{1}{2}$ teaspoon ground ginger

$\frac{1}{2}$ teaspoon ground cinnamon

$\frac{1}{2}$ teaspoon garlic powder

$\frac{1}{2}$ teaspoon cayenne pepper

$\frac{1}{2}$ teaspoon salt

3 tablespoons unsalted butter

3 quarts popped corn

In a nonstick skillet over medium heat, combine coriander seeds, cumin seeds, and peppercorns. Stir and toast until fragrant, about 2 minutes. Transfer coriander mixture to a spice mill, food processor, or blender. Add remaining ingredients except butter and popcorn; process to a smooth powder.

Preheat oven to 300° F. Melt butter in a small saucepan over low heat. Stir in coriander mixture. Cook, stirring, for 1 minute. Pour over popcorn; toss to coat evenly. Transfer popcorn to a large baking pan. Bake for 5 minutes, stirring once, until crisped. Store in an airtight container for up to 1 week.

MAKES ABOUT 3 QUARTS

Popcorn Yield

Popping volume varies for different kinds of popcorn, but generally two tablespoons unpopped popcorn kernels makes about 1 quart of popped corn.

JALAPEÑO PECAN

¼ cup (½ stick) unsalted butter

3 fresh jalapeño chiles, seeded and minced

2 teaspoons chili powder

½ teaspoon ground cumin

½ teaspoon garlic powder

½ teaspoon salt

1 cup pecan halves

2 quarts popped corn

In a large heavy skillet, melt butter over low heat. Add remaining ingredients except popcorn. Cook, stirring constantly, until pecans are toasted and fragrant, about 5 minutes. Pour over popcorn; toss to coat evenly. Store in an airtight container for up to 1 week.

MAKES ABOUT 2 QUARTS

JAMAICAN GINGER

3 tablespoons unsalted butter

½ tablespoon ground ginger

⅛ teaspoon ground cloves

½ teaspoon dried lemon peel

¼ teaspoon hot pepper sauce

½ teaspoon salt

2 quarts popped corn

In a small saucepan, melt butter over low heat. Add ginger and cook for 2 minutes. Stir in cloves, lemon peel, hot pepper sauce, and salt. Cook for 1 minute. Drizzle over popcorn. Toss to mix evenly. Store in an airtight container for up to 3 days.

MAKES ABOUT 2 ½ QUARTS

What Is Popcorn?

Of five varieties of corn, popcorn *(Zea mays everta)* is the kind that pops. Besides the more common yellow and white kernels, popcorn also comes in purple, rusty red, and black/blue—in fact, more than 1,300 kinds of popcorn have been developed by growers. But no matter what color the kernel is, the popped corn is always yellow or white.

LEMON BASIL

¼ cup (½ stick) unsalted butter

2 teaspoons dried lemon peel

1 tablespoon dried crushed basil

½ teaspoon onion powder

½ teaspoon garlic powder

½ teaspoon salt

3 quarts popped corn

In a small saucepan, melt butter over low heat. Add remaining ingredients except popcorn. Cook, stirring, for 1 minute. Drizzle herb butter over popcorn; mix well to coat evenly. Serve at once. Store in an airtight container for up to 1 week.

MAKES 3 QUARTS

Nacho

¼ cup (½ stick) unsalted butter

½ teaspoon ground cumin

1 ½ tablespoons ground New Mexican red chile
   or good-quality chili powder

½ teaspoon garlic powder

½ teaspoon onion powder

½ teaspoon crushed dried oregano

¼ teaspoon salt

3 quarts popped corn

1 cup (4 ounces) shredded jack cheese

1 cup (4 ounces) shredded sharp cheddar cheese

½ cup sliced ripe olives

Preheat oven to 300° F. In a small saucepan, melt butter over low heat. Add cumin, red chile, garlic powder, onion powder, oregano, and salt. Cook for 1 minute.

Place popcorn in a large shallow casserole. Drizzle butter mixture over popcorn; toss to coat evenly. Sprinkle with cheeses and olives. Bake for 15 minutes, stirring every 5 minutes, until cheese melts. Serve at once.

MAKES ABOUT 3 QUARTS

The Oldest Popcorn

During expeditions in 1948, ears of popcorn up to 2 inches long were found in Bat Cave in west central New Mexico by two Harvard graduate students, anthropologist Herbert Dick and botanist Earle Smith. The tiny ears have been identified by radio-carbon tests to be about 5,600 years old. Not only is this the oldest known corn in America, but the discovery proved popcorn to be the oldest known corn in the world as well.

Try Different Popping Oils

Since it has the lowest saturated fat content of all cooking oils and imparts no flavor of its own, canola oil is the preferred cooking oil to use for popping corn. For variety, you could also use a flavored monounsaturated oil such as olive, corn, peanut, or macadamia oil. If you like the flavor of toasted sesame seeds, add a few drops of dark sesame oil to canola oil for a highly flavored popping oil. Use the sesame oil sparingly because it has an intense flavor.

PIZZA

½ cup melted unsalted butter

3 tablespoons dry spaghetti sauce mix

(without mushrooms)

1 tablespoon crushed dried oregano

1 teaspoon garlic powder

3 quarts popped corn

Preheat oven to 250° F. In a small saucepan, melt butter over low heat. Add spaghetti sauce mix, oregano, and garlic powder. Cook, stirring, for 1 minute. Place popcorn in a large baking pan. Drizzle butter mixture over popcorn. Toss well to coat evenly. Bake for 5 minutes, stirring twice, until crisped. Store in an airtight container for up to 1 week.

MAKES ABOUT 3 QUARTS

RAGIN' CAJUN

3 tablespoons unsalted butter

¼ teaspoon dried minced garlic

1 teaspoon paprika

1 ½ teaspoons hot pepper sauce, or to taste

½ teaspoon cayenne pepper, or to taste

¼ teaspoon crushed dried oregano

¼ teaspoon crushed dried thyme

1 teaspoon salt

2 quarts popped corn

Preheat oven to 250° F. In a small saucepan, melt butter with remaining ingredients except popcorn over low heat. Cook, stirring constantly, for 2 minutes. Place popcorn in a large baking pan; drizzle butter mixture over popcorn, tossing well to coat evenly. Bake popcorn for 5 minutes, stirring twice, until crisped. Store in an airtight container for up to 1 week.

MAKES ABOUT 2 QUARTS

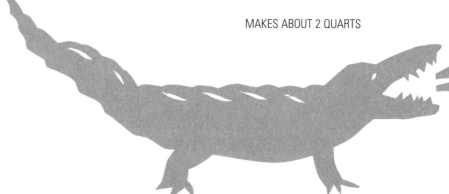

SANTA FE TRAIL MIX

¼ cup (½ stick) unsalted butter

½ teaspoon garlic powder

1 teaspoon ground cumin

¼ teaspoon hot red pepper flakes

¼ teaspoon salt

1 teaspoon grated lime zest

2 quarts popped corn

1 cup dry roasted peanuts

2 cups small corn chips

In a small saucepan, melt butter over low heat. Stir in garlic powder, cumin, hot pepper flakes, and salt. Cook, stirring, for 1 minute. Add lime zest. Pour over popped corn. Stir gently to coat evenly. Add dry roasted peanuts and corn chips; mix gently. Store in an airtight container for up to 3 days.

MAKES ABOUT 2 ½ QUARTS

Why Does Popcorn Pop?

Popcorn is made up principally of a starch that contains a small amount of moisture. When the kernels are heated, the water inside turns to steam and builds up pressure. The hard surface surrounding the starch eventually no longer can resist the building pressure and the popcorn explodes, turning the kernel inside out.

SESAME HOT CHILI

2 tablespoons sesame seeds

3 tablespoons unsalted butter

1 teaspoon dark sesame oil

½ tablespoon hot chili oil

¼ teaspoon garlic powder

2 tablespoons soy sauce

3 quarts popped corn

1 cup dry roasted cashews

In a small nonstick skillet, toast sesame seeds over medium-high heat, shaking pan occasionally, until seeds are golden and fragrant, about 3 to 4 minutes. Set seeds aside. In same skillet, melt butter over low heat. Add sesame oil, chili oil, garlic powder, and soy sauce. Blend well. Drizzle over popcorn; mix well. Add cashews and sesame seeds; mix again. Store in an airtight container for up to 3 days.

MAKES ABOUT 3 ¼ QUARTS

SUN-DRIED TOMATO

⅓ cup sun-dried tomatoes, packed in oil, drained

3 tablespoons olive oil

2 teaspoons dried mixed Italian herbs

½ teaspoon salt

3 tablespoons unsalted butter

3 quarts popped corn

In a food processor or blender, combine sun-dried tomatoes, olive oil, Italian herbs, and salt. Process to form a paste. In a small saucepan, melt butter over low heat. Stir in tomato paste. Mix well. Drizzle over popcorn and toss to coat evenly. Serve at once.

MAKES ABOUT 3 QUARTS

1,500-Year-Old Popcorn Poppers

By the time Europeans arrived in the New World, more than 700 varieties of popcorn were grown by Native American tribes in both Americas, except in the most northern and southern regions. Clay or metal cooking vessels were sometimes used—the Chicago Natural History Museum has a number of pre-Incan 1,500-year-old popcorn poppers.

Taco

¼ cup (½ stick) unsalted butter

3 tablespoons dry taco seasoning mix

1 teaspoon crushed dried oregano

1 teaspoon ground cumin

1 teaspoon garlic powder

3 quarts popped corn

Preheat oven to 250° F. In a small saucepan, melt butter over low heat. Stir in taco seasoning mix, oregano, cumin, and garlic powder. Place popcorn in a large baking pan. Drizzle with butter mixture; toss to coat evenly. Bake for 5 minutes, stirring twice, until hot and crispy. Store in an airtight container for up to 1 week.

MAKES ABOUT 3 QUARTS

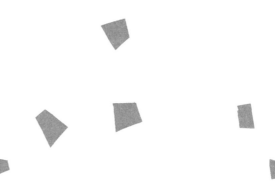

White Cheddar

¼ cup unsalted butter

½ teaspoon salt

2 quarts popped corn

2 cups (8 ounces) finely grated sharp white
  cheddar cheese

Preheat oven to 300° F. In a small saucepan over low heat, melt butter. Add salt. Place popcorn in a large baking pan. Drizzle with butter; sprinkle with cheese. Toss to coat evenly. Bake for 10 minutes, stirring twice, until cheese melts and popcorn is hot. Serve at once.

MAKES ABOUT 2 ½ QUARTS

Sweet Popcorn Confections

Popcorn Pointers

◆ Before measuring the popcorn, discard any unpopped kernels.

◆ Seasonings and sweet syrups will mix with the popcorn better if the popcorn is warm.

◆ When making sweet popcorn confections, choose a cool, dry day. Too much humidity will make the candy coating sticky.

◆ To avoid boilovers when making a candy syrup, lightly butter the inside of the saucepan before adding the ingredients.

◆ When baking soda is added to a candy syrup, the mixture will foam. Be sure to use the directed pan size to avoid messy boilover.

◆ When using a candy thermometer to make a syrup, be sure that the thermometer is not in contact with the bottom of the pan, or you'll be measuring the temperature of the pan and not that of the candy syrup.

◆ A wooden spoon is best for stirring a candy syrup.

BANANA PRALINE

1 ½ cups firmly packed light brown sugar
½ cup (1 stick) unsalted butter
1 teaspoon salt
1 teaspoon banana extract
3 quarts popped corn
2 cups dried banana slices

In a medium saucepan, combine sugar and butter. Place over medium heat and stir constantly until all sugar crystals are dissolved, about 5 minutes. Remove from heat and stir in salt and banana extract. Pour mixture over popcorn. Stir in banana slices. Transfer mixture to a large sheet of aluminum foil. Spread out evenly to cool. Break into small clusters. Store in an airtight container for up to 3 days.

MAKES ABOUT 3 ½ QUARTS

BETTER-THAN-JACK

> ¼ cup (½ stick) unsalted butter
>
> 1 ½ cups granulated sugar
>
> ½ cup light corn syrup
>
> ½ cup molasses
>
> 2 tablespoons white distilled vinegar
>
> ½ teaspoon salt
>
> ½ teaspoon baking soda
>
> ½ cup walnuts
>
> ½ cup pecans
>
> ½ cup whole almonds
>
> ½ cup hazelnuts
>
> 2 quarts popped corn

In a medium saucepan, melt butter over low heat. Stir in sugar, corn syrup, molasses, vinegar, and salt. Bring to a boil, stirring constantly. Reduce heat and gently boil until the mixture reaches 260° F on a candy thermometer. Remove from heat; stir in baking soda and nuts. Pour over popcorn, stirring gently to coat evenly. Transfer mixture to a large sheet of aluminum foil. Cool and separate small clusters. Store in an airtight container for up to 1 week.

MAKES ABOUT 4 QUARTS

"Get Your Cracker Jack Here..."

Since 1896, when the Rueckheim brothers of Chicago added molasses and peanuts to popcorn, and since 1908, when the caramelized popcorn was lyricized in the song "Take Me Out to the Ball Game," Cracker Jack has been a favorite of children all over the world. The yummy version offered here has a combination of four kinds of nuts as the special prize.

BUTTERSCOTCH TOFFEE

½ cup (1 stick) unsalted butter

¼ cup heavy cream

1 ½ cups firmly packed light brown sugar

1 teaspoon vanilla extract

1 12-ounce package butterscotch morsels

3 quarts popped corn

In a large saucepan, combine butter, cream, sugar, vanilla, and butterscotch morsels. Bring to a boil, stirring constantly, over medium heat. Reduce heat to low and cook, stirring constantly, until butterscotch mixture reaches 280° F on a candy thermometer. Pour mixture over popcorn; toss gently to coat evenly. Store in an airtight container for up to 3 days.

MAKES ABOUT 3 QUARTS

Candy Thermometers

Most of the sweet popcorn recipes call for the use of a candy thermometer to keep the guesswork out of making the sweet coating. It's a good idea to occasionally check the accuracy of your candy thermometer by letting it stand for 10 minutes in boiling water. The thermometer should read 212° F. If there's any variation, subtract or add to make the same degree of allowance when testing the candied syrup.

CALIFORNIA COMBO

2 quarts popped corn
1 cup whole almonds
1 cup seedless raisins
1 12-ounce package white chocolate morsels

In a large bowl, toss together popcorn, almonds, and raisins. In a 1-quart glass measuring cup, microwave chocolate pieces on HIGH for 3 minutes, stirring after each minute, until melted. Remove from microwave and stir until smooth. Pour over popcorn, almonds, and raisins. Stir to coat evenly. Transfer mixture to a large sheet of aluminum foil. When cool, break into small clusters. Store in an airtight container for up to 1 week.

MAKES ABOUT 2 ½ QUARTS

Variation: Substitute mint chocolate chips for white chocolate chips.

CARAMEL FUDGE

1 14-ounce package light caramel candies
2 tablespoons heavy cream
3 quarts popped corn
1 6-ounce package semisweet chocolate morsels

In a 3-quart microwave-safe casserole, combine caramel squares and heavy cream. Cover with lid or plastic wrap. Microwave on HIGH for 3 minutes, stirring after every minute, until mixture comes to a boil.

Pour caramel sauce over popcorn, stirring to coat evenly. Quickly stir in semisweet chocolate morsels. Transfer mixture to a large sheet of aluminum foil. When cool, break into small clusters. Store in an airtight container for up to 1 week.

MAKES ABOUT 3 ½ QUARTS

CARAMEL PEANUT

½ cup unsalted butter

1 cup firmly packed brown sugar

¼ cup light corn syrup

½ teaspoon salt

¼ teaspoon baking soda

½ teaspoon vanilla extract

3 quarts popped corn

2 cups dry roasted peanuts

Preheat oven to 250° F. In a medium saucepan, melt butter over low heat. Add brown sugar, corn syrup, and salt. Bring mixture to a boil, stirring constantly. Gently boil without stirring for 5 minutes. Remove from heat; add baking soda and vanilla extract. Stir until smooth.

Place popcorn in a large, lightly buttered baking pan. Pour syrup over popcorn and toss to coat evenly. Stir in peanuts. Bake for 1 hour, stirring every 15 minutes. Remove from oven; cool. Break popcorn into small clusters. Store in an airtight container for up to 1 week.

MAKES ABOUT 3 QUARTS

Easy Sweetened Popcorn

When popping in oil, add a tablespoon of sugar just as the corn begins to pop for a delicate, sweet flavor. Once the sugar is added, quickly recover the popper and continue popping.

Linda's Christmas Popcorn Cake

The first Christmas she lived in South Carolina, herbalist Linda Fleming received several popcorn cakes as housewarming gifts, a holiday tradition throughout the South. Although she and her family now reside in Connecticut, Christmas is not complete until the popcorn cake is made.

Linda's rich version is sure to delight children and adults alike: In a large bowl, combine 8 cups popped corn, 10 ounces small assorted colored gumdrops, and 2 cups salted peanuts. In a medium saucepan, melt together ½ cup (1 stick) butter or margarine, ½ cup canola oil, and 1 pound marshmallows. Stir until well blended. Pour over popcorn mixture and carefully stir until evenly coated. Lightly pack into a buttered angel food or bundt cake pan. Let cool completely, about 6 hours. Remove from pan and sprinkle with colored sugar. To serve, slice thinly.

MAKES 10-12 SERVINGS

CHOCOLATE CRUNCH

1 quart popped corn

2 cups very small bow-knot pretzels

1 cup Virginia peanuts

1 12-ounce package semisweet chocolate morsels

In a large bowl, combine popcorn, pretzels, and peanuts. Place chocolate morsels in a 1-quart glass measuring cup. Microwave on HIGH for 1 minute; stir. Continue to cook on HIGH for another minute; stir again. Cook on HIGH for an additional 15 seconds and pour chocolate over popcorn mixture. Stir to coat evenly. Spread mixture on a large baking sheet lined with aluminum foil. Place in refrigerator for 15 to 20 minutes, until chilled and chocolate is set. Break into small clusters. Store in an airtight container for up to 1 week.

MAKES ABOUT 2 QUARTS

Cinnamon

1 cup granulated sugar

½ cup water

1 tablespoon distilled white vinegar

3 tablespoons molasses

¼ cup (½ stick) unsalted butter

½ teaspoon salt

5 drops red food coloring

1 teaspoon cinnamon oil

2 quarts popped corn

In a heavy saucepan, combine sugar, water, and vinegar. Bring to a boil over medium-high heat; stir often until sugar dissolves. Stir in molasses, butter, and salt. Gently boil, stirring occasionally, until mixture reaches 280° F on a candy thermometer. Remove from heat and stir in red food coloring and cinnamon oil. Quickly pour syrup over popcorn; gently stir to coat evenly. Let cool until syrup is no longer sticky. Break into small clusters. Store in an airtight container for up to 3 days.

MAKES ABOUT 2 QUARTS

Popcorn in the New World

Christophor Columbus is credited with introducing popcorn to Europe after his return from the West Indies, where he had found the natives eating popcorn and wearing it as decoration, like corsages.

Cortés got his first glimpse of popcorn when he invaded Mexico in 1519 and came into contact with the Aztecs, who used popcorn to decorate ceremonial headdresses and strung it into necklaces.

In 1650, the Spanish explorer Cobo wrote of Peruvian Indians using a kind of corn as a confection that when toasted, burst.

Popcorn at the First Thanksgiving?

According to the popular legend, English colonists were introduced to popcorn when Quadequina, brother of the Wampanoag chief Massasoit, brought a deerskin bag of popped corn to the first Thanksgiving feast at Plymouth, Massachusetts.

However, it's more likely that parched flint corn (the multicolored corn also called Indian corn that's often used for decoration) was brought to the feast. According to historians at Plimouth Plantation, Plymouth, Massachusetts, flint corn, and not popcorn, was the native corn of the region. Parching explodes the corn kernel partially, making it edible but not as tasty as popcorn.

"Parched corn" is also referred to in several historical writings by Governor John Winthrop of Connecticut and a century later by Benjamin Franklin.

CRANBERRY

¼ cup (½ stick) unsalted butter
1 cup granulated sugar
¼ cup light corn syrup
6 ounces frozen cranberry juice concentrate,
 thawed
3 quarts popped corn
1 cup dried cranberries

In a small saucepan, melt butter over low heat. Stir in sugar, corn syrup, and cranberry juice concentrate. Bring to a boil, stirring constantly. Lower heat and simmer until mixture reaches 285° F on a candy thermometer.

Place popcorn and dried cranberries in a large bowl. Pour syrup over popcorn and stir until well coated. Spread popcorn evenly on a large sheet of aluminum foil; let cool completely. Break into small clusters. Store in an airtight container for up to 1 week.

MAKES ABOUT 3 QUARTS

GRAPE

3 quarts popped corn

¼ cup (½ stick) unsalted butter

1 cup granulated sugar

¼ cup light corn syrup

6 ounces frozen grape juice concentrate,
   thawed

½ teaspoon salt

½ teaspoon vanilla extract

Preheat oven to 250° F. Place popcorn in a large baking pan. In a medium saucepan, melt butter over low heat. Stir in sugar, corn syrup, and grape juice concentrate. Bring to a boil, stirring constantly. Reduce heat and gently boil, stirring occasionally, until mixture reaches 285° F on a candy thermometer. Remove from heat. Stir in salt and vanilla extract. Pour syrup over popcorn and gently stir to coat evenly. Bake for 5 minutes, stirring after 3 minutes. Remove from oven and cool. Break into small clusters. Store in an airtight container for up to 1 week.

MAKES ABOUT 3 QUARTS

Honey Almond Crunch

2 quarts popped corn
1 cup sliced almonds
$\frac{3}{4}$ cup honey
$\frac{1}{3}$ cup unsalted butter
$\frac{1}{2}$ teaspoon salt
1 teaspoon almond extract

Preheat oven to 250° F. Place popcorn and almonds in a large baking pan. In a 1-quart glass measuring cup, combine honey and butter. Microwave on HIGH for 2 minutes, stirring after 1 minute. Remove from oven and stir in salt and almond extract. Pour syrup over popcorn and gently stir to coat evenly. Bake for 5 minutes, stirring after 3 minutes. Remove from oven and transfer popcorn to a large sheet of aluminum foil to cool. Break into small clusters. Store in an airtight container for up to 1 week.

MAKES ABOUT 2 QUARTS

Growing Popcorn

Popcorn is easy and fun to grow. Plant blocks of short rows, 30 inches apart, in a sunny location after the soil is warm and the danger of a last frost is past. Plant the seeds well away from where you are growing sweet corn to avoid possible cross-pollination. When plants are about a foot tall, pile additional soil around the base of the stalks.

When corn is 6 inches tall, and again at mid-season, apply a high-nitrogen fertilizer. Water regularly until plants are well established. Then water less often, but deeply, to encourage strong root systems. Do not let soil dry out, especially when the ears are developing, or they will only partially fill. Mulch to keep weeds down and to conserve water.

Let ears mature fully before harvesting. When the stalks and husks are completely brown and kernels are hard (test by sticking your thumb nail into a kernel—it shouldn't make a dent), the popcorn is ready to harvest, dry, and store. Once picked, peel back the husks to aid drying and hang the ears in a dry, airy spot. When kernels can be shucked off the cob easily, try popping a few kernels (at least 8 out of 10 kernels should pop). If the popcorn is still too wet, the popped kernels will be mushy and chewy. To shell the popcorn, hold the ear with the husk end in one hand. Twist the other hand to free the kernels, moving up the ear. Once shelled, separate the chaff and pieces of dried silk from the kernels.

Store the kernels in sealed glass jars until ready to use (wait at least two weeks after shelling before popping). You should get about ¼ cup of kernels from each ear of medium-sized popcorn variety.

HONEY ORANGE

2 quarts popped corn
1 cup chopped walnuts
½ cup honey, preferably orange
¼ cup (½ stick) unsalted butter
½ teaspoon salt
1 tablespoon dried orange peel

Preheat oven to 250° F. Place popcorn and walnuts in a large baking pan. Set aside. In a small saucepan, combine honey and butter. Bring to a boil; cook for 1 minute. Remove from stove and stir in salt and dried orange peel. Pour honey mixture over popcorn; gently stir to coat evenly. Bake for 5 minutes, stirring after 3 minutes. Remove from oven and cool. Break into small clusters. Store in an airtight container for up to 1 week.

MAKES ABOUT 2 QUARTS

KEY LIME

3 quarts popped corn
¼ cup (½ stick) unsalted butter
1 cup granulated sugar
½ cup light corn syrup
1 cup bottled key lime juice
2 tablespoons heavy cream
1 tablespoon grated fresh lime zest

Preheat oven to 250° F. Place popcorn in a large baking pan. In a medium saucepan, melt butter over low heat. Stir in sugar, corn syrup, key lime juice, and heavy cream. Bring to a boil, stirring constantly. Reduce heat and gently boil, stirring occasionally, until mixture reaches 285° F on a candy thermometer. Remove from heat. Stir in lime zest. Pour syrup over popcorn and gently stir to coat evenly. Bake for 5 minutes, stirring after 3 minutes. Remove from oven and cool. Break into small clusters. Store in an airtight container for up to 3 days.

MAKES ABOUT 2 QUARTS

MACADAMIA BUTTER CRUNCH

2 quarts popped corn

1 3 ½-ounce jar macadamia nuts

¾ cup firmly packed light brown sugar

3 tablespoons light corn syrup

⅓ cup unsalted butter

½ teaspoon salt

½ teaspoon baking soda

½ teaspoon vanilla extract

Preheat oven to 250° F. Place popcorn and macadamia nuts in a large baking pan. Set aside. In a 1½-quart microwave-safe casserole, stir together sugar and corn syrup. Microwave on HIGH for 6 minutes, stirring after 3 minutes. Stir in butter. Microwave on HIGH for 1 minute. Remove from oven and stir in salt, baking soda, and vanilla extract. Pour syrup over popcorn; stir gently to coat evenly. Bake for 5 minutes, stirring after 3 minutes. Remove from oven and transfer popcorn mixture to a large sheet of aluminum foil to cool. Break into small clusters. Store in an airtight container for up to 1 week.

MAKES ABOUT 2 QUARTS

All Popcorn Has Hulls

Although some popcorn packagers call their popcorn "hull-less," all popcorn has hulls. Without the thin, hard covering around the kernel that shatters when the kernel is heated and explodes, popcorn wouldn't pop. Today's popcorn is bred so that the hull explodes with more force, shattering it into tiny fragments, making the popcorn appear to be hull-less.

MAPLE TOASTED PECAN

1 ½ cups pecans
1 ½ cups maple syrup
¼ cup (½ stick) unsalted butter
½ teaspoon salt
2 quarts popped corn

Preheat oven to 300° F. Spread pecans in a baking pan. Toast for 5 minutes, shaking pan occasionally, until pecans are fragrant and crispy.

Combine maple syrup and butter in a medium saucepan. Bring to a boil, stirring constantly. Continue to cook, stirring, until a candy thermometer registers 270° F. Stir in salt.

In a large bowl, combine popcorn and pecans. Slowly pour hot syrup over popcorn; stir gently to coat evenly. Transfer mixture to a large sheet of aluminum foil. Cool completely. Break into small clusters. Store in an airtight container for up to 1 week.

MAKES ABOUT 2 ½ QUARTS

Mocha Almond

1 6-ounce package semisweet chocolate morsels
¼ cup (½ stick) unsalted butter
¼ cup light corn syrup
½ cup confectioner's sugar
1 tablespoon powdered instant espresso
1 teaspoon almond extract
1 quart popped corn
½ cup sliced almonds

In a 3-quart microwave casserole, stir together chocolate morsels, butter, and corn syrup. Cook on HIGH 3 to 4 minutes, stirring after 2 minutes, until chocolate is melted and mixture is smooth. Stir in confectioner's sugar, instant espresso, and almond extract. Add popcorn and almonds. Stir to coat evenly. Transfer popcorn mixture to a large sheet of aluminum foil. Cool completely; break into small clusters. Store in an airtight container for up to 3 days.

MAKES ABOUT 1 ¼ QUARTS

Peanut Butter Crunch

½ cup sugar
½ cup light corn syrup
½ teaspoon vanilla extract
½ cup chunky-style peanut butter
1 cup dry roasted peanuts
2 quarts popped corn

Heat sugar and corn syrup in a medium saucepan over medium-high heat, stirring constantly until sugar is dissolved, about 5 minutes. Bring to a rolling boil.

Remove from heat; stir in vanilla extract, peanut butter, and peanuts. Pour over popcorn and toss. Store in an airtight container for up to 1 week.

MAKES ABOUT 2 ¼ QUARTS

Popcorn Lingo

Old Maids: The unpopped kernels remaining on the bottom of the popper after the corn is popped. For a more complete pop, store unpopped popcorn in an airtight jar—but not in the refrigerator.

Snowflakes and Mushrooms: The terms used to describe the shapes of popped corn. "Snowflakes" pop big and have the shape of a cumulus cloud; "mushrooms" are almost round like a ball. The ratio of "snowflakes" to "mushrooms" depends on the type of popcorn.

Rice and Pearls: The two major types of popcorn grown commercially. "Rice" has sharply pointed kernels and "pearls" have smooth rounded crowns.

More Snowflakes

In the 1960's a county extension agent in Indiana named Orville Redenbacher developed a hybrid popcorn seed that produced a "snowflake" variety with a higher popping volume and fewer unpoppable kernels than other kinds of popping corn. He marketed his "gourmet popping corn" from the back of a car until the company was bought in 1974.

PECAN ALMOND PRALINE

2 cups firmly packed light brown sugar

¾ cup whipping cream

1 tablespoon butter

½ teaspoon salt

1 cup pecans

1 cup sliced almonds

3 quarts popped corn

In a heavy saucepan, combine brown sugar, cream, butter, and salt. Cook, stirring constantly, until sugar is dissolved. Continue to cook, stirring occasionally, until mixture reaches 240° F on a candy thermometer, about 20 minutes. Remove from heat and cool for 5 minutes. Stir until mixture coats a spoon.

In a large bowl, combine pecans, almonds, and popcorn. Pour sugar mixture over popcorn; stir to coat evenly. Transfer popcorn to a large sheet of aluminum foil. When cool, break into small clusters. Store in an airtight container for up to 3 days.

MAKES ABOUT 2 ½ QUARTS

PIÑA COLADA

1 ½ cups shredded coconut

⅓ cup unsalted butter

1 cup granulated sugar

¼ cup light corn syrup

6 ounces frozen piña colada mix, thawed

1 teaspoon rum extract

2 quarts popped corn

1 cup diced dried pineapple

Preheat broiler. Place coconut in a large baking pan and toast until golden, about 3 minutes, stirring frequently. (Be careful—coconut browns very quickly.) Set aside. In a heavy saucepan, melt butter over low heat. Stir in sugar, corn syrup, and piña colada mix. Bring to a boil, stirring constantly. Reduce heat and simmer until mixture reaches 280° F on a candy thermometer. Remove from heat and stir in rum extract.

In a large bowl, combine popcorn, toasted coconut, and dried pineapple. Pour over syrup mixture. Stir to coat evenly. Spread popcorn on a large sheet of aluminum foil to cool. Break into small clusters. Store in an airtight container for up to 1 week.

MAKES ABOUT 2 QUARTS

PINEAPPLE MACADAMIA

⅓ cup unsalted butter

1 cup granulated sugar

½ cup light corn syrup

1 6-ounce can frozen pineapple juice concentrate,
thawed

¼ cup heavy cream

2 quarts popped corn

1 cup diced dried pineapple

1 3 ½-ounce jar macadamia nuts

In a heavy saucepan, melt butter over medium-high heat. Stir in sugar, corn syrup, pineapple juice concentrate, and heavy cream. Bring to a boil, stirring constantly. Reduce heat and gently boil, without stirring, until mixture reaches 280° F on a candy thermometer. Pour syrup over popcorn and gently stir to coat evenly. Stir in pineapple and nuts. Transfer mixture to a large sheet of aluminum foil to cool. Break into small clusters. Store in an airtight container for up to 3 days.

MAKES ABOUT 2 ½ QUARTS

ROCKY ROAD POPCORN BALLS

1 cup light corn syrup

1 cup granulated sugar

1 tablespoon white vinegar

2 tablespoons water

½ teaspoon salt

¼ cup (½ stick) butter

1 teaspoon vanilla extract

½ teaspoon baking soda

3 quarts popped corn

1 ½ cups miniature marshmallows

1 cup salted peanuts

1 6-ounce package butterscotch morsels

1 6-ounce package semisweet chocolate morsels

Unsalted butter for rolling

In a large heavy saucepan, combine corn syrup, sugar, vinegar, water, and salt. Bring to a boil and cook over medium-high heat, stirring occasionally, until mixture reaches 230° F on a candy thermometer. Stir in butter and continue cooking, stirring occasionally, until mixture reaches 260° F. Remove from heat and stir in vanilla extract and soda.

Place popcorn in a large bowl. Pour syrup over popcorn; stir to coat completely. Quickly add marshmallows, peanuts, butterscotch morsels, and chocolate morsels. Stir well. Using buttered hands to prevent sticking, quickly form mixture into small balls. Cool on a sheet of aluminum foil. Wrap each ball in plastic wrap; will keep for up to 1 week.

MAKES ABOUT 16 3-INCH BALLS

Guinness Book of World Records

The world's largest popcorn ball, measuring 12 feet in diameter, was conceived and constructed by Chef Franz Eichenauer, a professor of culinary arts, in 1981 to raise funds for the Peekskill, New York, Area Health Center. The ball used more than 2,000 pounds of popcorn and was popped by the Borden Company, mixed with 4,000 pounds of sugar, 280 gallons of corn syrup, and 400 gallons of water.

Swags of Popcorn

Stringing swags of popcorn for the Christmas tree has been a tradition in my home since early childhood. The swags are particularly lovely when slices of air-dried orange, lemon, and apple are interspersed with the popcorn. Fresh cranberries and cinnamon sticks alternated with popcorn makes a festive—and fragrant—festoon as well. Once the holiday is over, hang the swags in outdoor fir trees as a gift to the birds.

SASSY LEMON

⅓ cup unsalted butter

1 cup granulated sugar

¼ cup light corn syrup

¼ teaspoon salt

¼ teaspoon baking soda

1 tablespoon dried lemon peel

2 quarts popped corn

Preheat oven to 250° F. In a medium saucepan, melt butter over low heat. Stir in sugar, corn syrup, and salt. Bring to a boil, stirring constantly. Reduce heat to simmer and cook until mixture reaches 250° F on a candy thermometer. Remove from heat. Stir in baking soda and dried lemon peel. Pour over popcorn and mix well to coat evenly. Spread popcorn evenly in a large baking pan. Bake for 10 minutes, stirring after 5 minutes. Remove from oven and cool completely. Break into small clusters. Store in an airtight container for up to 1 week.

MAKES ABOUT 2 QUARTS

Southern Bourbon Brittle

2 quarts popped corn
2 cups pecan halves
5 tablespoons unsalted butter
1 cup firmly packed dark brown sugar
⅔ cup dark corn syrup
½ cup good-quality bourbon

In a large bowl, combine popcorn and pecans. In a small saucepan over medium heat, combine butter with remaining ingredients. Bring to a boil over medium heat, stirring until sugar dissolves. Reduce heat to low and continue to cook, stirring occasionally, until mixture reaches 275° F on a candy thermometer. Pour syrup over popcorn mixture; toss well to coat evenly. Spread on a large sheet of aluminum foil and cool completely. Break into small clusters.

MAKES 2 ½ QUARTS

SPICED APPLE

2 quarts popped corn

1 ½ cups sliced almonds

3 tablespoons unsalted butter

½ cup light corn syrup

½ cup frozen apple juice concentrate, thawed

½ cup firmly packed light brown sugar

½ teaspoon ground nutmeg

¼ teaspoon allspice

¼ teaspoon ground cloves

1 teaspoon salt

In a large mixing bowl, combine popcorn and almonds. In a small saucepan, combine remaining ingredients over medium heat. Stir until brown sugar dissolves. Reduce heat to low and continue to cook, stirring occasionally, until mixture forms a syrup and reaches 285° F on a candy thermometer. Pour syrup over popcorn mixture; toss well to coat evenly. Spread evenly on a large sheet of aluminum foil. When cool, break into small clumps. Store in an airtight container for up to 1 week.

MAKES 2 ½ QUARTS

Toasted Cinnamon Corn, Fruit, and Nut Jumble

2 quarts popped corn

1 cup coarsely chopped dried apricots

1 cup golden raisins

1 cup coarsely chopped walnuts

$\frac{1}{2}$ cup (1 stick) unsalted butter

1 cup sugar

$\frac{1}{4}$ cup water

$\frac{1}{2}$ tablespoon ground cinnamon

Preheat oven to 250° F. In a large baking pan, combine popcorn, apricots, raisins, and walnuts. Set aside.

In a small saucepan, melt butter over medium heat. Stir in sugar, water, and cinnamon. Simmer, stirring occasionally, until mixture reaches 250° F on a candy thermometer. Pour mixture over popcorn and stir to coat evenly. Bake for 15 minutes, stirring after every 5 minutes, until popcorn is toasted. Transfer mixture to a large sheet of aluminum foil; let cool at room temperature. Store in an airtight container for up to 1 week.

MAKES ABOUT 3 QUARTS

Harvest Celebrations

From Ohio to Nebraska—all the centers of popcorn production—
there are festivals and fairs celebrating the late-summer popcorn
harvest: Valparaiso, Indiana; Marion, Ohio; Ord, Nebraska; Schaller,
Iowa; Van Buren, Indiana; Hamburg, Iowa; and Ridgway, Illinois.
For information and precise date, write to the local chamber of
commerce.

First Popping Machine

In 1885, Charles Cretors of Chicago, Illinois, invented the first popping machine, powered by steam—an invention that revolutionized the industry. When he took his first popcorn wagon to Chicago's Columbian Exposition in 1893, lines of customers formed to watch the little red-suited clown perched atop the popcorn popper cranking away to keep up with the demand for the new snack—popcorn in butter.

At the same exhibition, Thomas A. Edison demonstrated his prototype movie projector. However, it wasn't until the mid-1930's that theater owners allowed the sale of popcorn (a nickel a box) on their premises. The once-familiar sight of sidewalk salesmen, pushing and driving popcorn wagons, faded from the American scene.

TOFFEE FUDGE CRUNCH

1 cup granulated sugar

½ cup light corn syrup

¼ cup (½ stick) unsalted butter

¼ cup whipping cream

1 teaspoon vanilla extract

2 quarts popped corn

4 1.4-ounce chocolate-toffee candy bars,

　　coarsely chopped

In a medium saucepan, combine sugar, corn syrup, butter, and whipping cream. Place over medium-high heat; stir until sugar dissolves. Continue to boil gently, without stirring, until mixture reaches 280° F on a candy thermometer. Stir in vanilla extract.

Place popcorn and chopped candy bars in a large bowl. Slowly pour over syrup, stirring gently until evenly coated. Transfer mixture to a large sheet of aluminum foil. Cool until syrup is no longer sticky. Break into small clusters. Store in an airtight container for up to 3 days.

MAKES ABOUT 2 ½ QUARTS

TUTTI-FRUTTI:
CHERRY, BLUEBERRY,
AND LIME

3 quarts popped corn

1 ½ cups light corn syrup

¾ cup granulated sugar

3 tablespoons cherry-flavored gelatin

3 tablespoons lime-flavored gelatin

3 tablespoons blueberry-flavored gelatin

Divide popcorn equally into 3 medium bowls. In a small saucepan over high heat, combine ½ cup corn syrup and ¼ cup sugar. Bring to a boil; cook for 1 minute. Add cherry-flavored gelatin, stirring until gelatin is dissolved. Pour syrup mixture into first bowl of popcorn. Stir to coat evenly. Transfer mixture to a sheet of aluminum foil to cool.

Repeat process, using lime-flavored gelatin. Pour over second bowl of popcorn. Stir to coat evenly. Transfer mixture to a sheet of aluminum foil to cool.

Repeat process, using blueberry-flavored gelatin. Pour over third bowl of popcorn. Stir to coat evenly. Transfer mixture to a sheet of aluminum foil to cool. When popcorn is thoroughly cool, break into small clusters and combine all three flavors. Store in an airtight container for up to 1 week.

MAKES ABOUT 3 QUARTS

Vanilla Candy Crunch

1 cup granulated sugar

$\frac{1}{2}$ cup light corn syrup

$\frac{1}{4}$ cup ($\frac{1}{2}$ stick) unsalted butter

$\frac{1}{2}$ teaspoon salt

$\frac{1}{4}$ cup whipping cream

1 tablespoon vanilla extract

2 quarts popped corn

2 cups candy-coated almond and milk chocolate pieces

In a medium saucepan, combine sugar, corn syrup, butter, salt, and cream. Bring to a boil over medium-high heat, stirring constantly. Continue to gently boil, without stirring, until mixture reaches 280° F on a candy thermometer. Remove from heat and stir in vanilla extract. Pour syrup over popcorn and stir gently until evenly coated. Transfer popcorn to a large sheet of aluminum foil to cool. Break into small clusters. Combine with candy pieces. Store in an airtight container for up to 1 week.

MAKES ABOUT 2 $\frac{1}{2}$ QUARTS

Skinny Popcorn Combinations

CHEESE AND PEPPER POPCORN

1 quart air-popped corn or corn popped with
no more than 1 teaspoon canola oil
Butter-flavored cooking spray or reconstituted
butter-flavored granules
¼ cup grated Parmesan cheese
⅛ teaspoon cayenne pepper

Preheat oven to 300° F. Spread popcorn on a nonstick cookie sheet and lightly spray with cooking spray. Sprinkle with cheese and cayenne pepper. Toss to coat evenly. Spray and toss again. Bake for 10 minutes, tossing once. Serve warm.

MAKES 1 SERVING

218 calories, 7 grams fat, 466 milligrams sodium
(258 calories, 12 grams fat, 466 milligrams sodium,
if popped with 1 teaspoon canola oil)

Skinny Tips

Popcorn prepared with butter-flavored cooking spray or reconstituted butter-flavored granules becomes soggy after a few hours. To enjoy it at its best, make the popcorn in small batches and eat it, freshly made, while it's still warm.

Popcorn on the Cob

In the fall of 1897, the Sears, Roebuck & Company catalog advertised a paper sack filled with 25 pounds of popping corn, sold on the cob (approximately 125 cobs), for one dollar. Now you can buy popping corn on the cob at specialty food stores, packaged with a microwave bag for popping the corn while still on the cob. Today's retail price for one cob of popcorn with a microwave popping bag is about $2.50.

GARLIC LOVER'S DELIGHT

*1 quart air-popped corn or corn popped with
no more than 1 teaspoon canola oil
Butter-flavored cooking spray or reconstituted
butter-flavored granules
2 teaspoons garlic powder
½ teaspoon onion powder
¼ teaspoon orange peel
Dash cayenne pepper*

Put popcorn in a large bowl and lightly spray with cooking spray. In a small bowl, combine remaining ingredients. Sprinkle over popcorn; toss to coat evenly. Spray and toss again until mixture is well coated. Serve at once.

MAKES 1 SERVING

116 calories, trace fat, 1 milligram sodium

(156 calories, 5 grams fat, 1 milligram sodium, if popped with 1 teaspoon canola oil)

GINGERSNAP POPCORN

1 quart air-popped corn or corn popped with
   no more than 1 teaspoon canola oil
Butter-flavored cooking spray or reconstituted
   butter-flavored granules
$\frac{1}{4}$ cup granulated sugar substitute
1 $\frac{1}{2}$ teaspoons ground ginger
$\frac{1}{2}$ teaspoon ground nutmeg
$\frac{1}{4}$ teaspoon ground cloves

Preheat oven to 300° F. Spread popcorn on a nonstick cookie sheet and lightly spray with cooking spray. In a small bowl, combine remaining ingredients. Sprinkle over popcorn; toss to coat evenly. Spray and toss again. Bake for 10 minutes, tossing once. Serve warm.

MAKES 1 SERVING

135 calories, < 1 gram fat, 2 milligrams sodium

(175 calories, 5 grams fat, 2 milligrams sodium, if popped with 1 teaspoon canola oil)

America's First Brand Name Popcorn

In 1914, an Iowa farmer, Choid H. Smith, founded the American Pop Corn Company in Sioux City, Iowa, and created America's first brand name popcorn—Jolly Time. A 1921 sales sheet shows the retail price of a 16-ounce box of extra-select popcorn kernels to be 10 cents.

The first airtight packaging for popcorn was introduced by Smith in 1924, a metal can that would prove to be the forerunner to today's soft drink cans.

In the 1930's, Jolly Time sponsored a national Sunday evening radio show that featured live orchestra music by General Jolly Time and his Pop Corn Colonels with a theme song titled "A Bowl of Pop Corn, a Radio, and You."

HUNAN POPCORN

1 quart air-popped corn or corn popped with
    no more than 1 teaspoon canola oil
Butter-flavored cooking spray or reconstituted
    butter-flavored granules
1 tablespoon low-sodium soy sauce
1 tablespoon lemon juice
$\frac{1}{8}$ teaspoon freshly ground pepper
1 teaspoon five-spice powder
$\frac{1}{4}$ teaspoon ground coriander
$\frac{1}{4}$ teaspoon garlic powder

Preheat oven to 250° F. Spread popcorn on a nonstick cookie sheet and lightly spray with cooking spray. In a glass measuring cup, microwave remaining ingredients on HIGH for 30 seconds. Stir and continue to microwave on HIGH for another 15 seconds. Drizzle over popcorn. Toss to coat evenly. Bake for 10 minutes, tossing once. Serve warm.

MAKES 1 SERVING

125 calories, trace fat, 530 milligrams sodium
(165 calories, 5 grams fat, 530 milligrams sodium,
if popped with 1 teaspoon canola oil)

LOW-FAT CHOCOLATE
POPCORN

1 quart air-popped corn or corn popped with
no more than 1 teaspoon canola oil
Butter-flavored cooking spray or reconstituted
butter-flavored granules
3 tablespoons powdered cocoa mix, already
sweetened with sugar substitute
1 teaspoon cinnamon

Put popcorn in a large bowl and lightly spray with cooking spray. Sprinkle cocoa mix and cinnamon on popcorn; toss to coat evenly. Spray and toss again until mixture is well coated. Serve at once.

MAKES 1 SERVING

208 calories, < 1 gram fat, 143 milligrams sodium
(248 calories, 5 grams fat, 143 milligrams sodium, if popped with 1 teaspoon canola oil)

MEXICAN POPCORN

1 quart air-popped corn or corn popped with no more
than 1 teaspoon canola oil
Butter-flavored cooking spray or reconstituted butter-
flavored granules
1 tablespoon dried Mexican spiced salad dressing mix
½ teaspoon crushed dried oregano
½ teaspoon crushed dried thyme
¼ teaspoon garlic powder

Put popcorn in a large bowl and lightly spray with cooking spray. In a small bowl, combine remaining ingredients. Sprinkle over popcorn. Toss to coat evenly. Spray and toss again. Serve at once.

MAKES 1 SERVING

108 calories, trace fat, 87 milligrams sodium

(148 calories, 5 grams fat, 87 milligrams sodium if popped with 1 teaspoon canola oil)

Popcorn Flour

A very light flour with the delicate flavor of popcorn, popcorn flour contains 80 to 120 calories per cup versus 400 to 420 calories per cup of whole wheat or white all-purpose flour. Although you can buy popcorn flour in specialty food stores, you can easily make it yourself.

To make 1 cup of popcorn flour, whirl 2 cups unbuttered hot-air-popped corn in a food processor or blender to form a fine powder. Use the flour in your favorite recipes, substituting 1¼ cups popcorn flour for 1 cup whole wheat flour or 1 cup white all-purpose flour, replacing no more than ⅓ of the total amount of flour in each recipe.

Popcorn Gifts

Be on the look-out throughout the year for nifty containers that you can fill with popcorn and give as gifts. Choose a simple or whimsical container (it must be scrubbed clean and dried; some will need a zip-lock bag liner to preserve freshness) and adorn it for the occasion. Especially nice for popcorn:

- ◆ Printed or metallic cardboard gift box
- ◆ Glass or plastic jar with cork stopper or brightly colored lid
- ◆ Small metal or plastic bucket
- ◆ Metal decorated tins
- ◆ New Chinese take-out food containers
- ◆ Paper shopping bag or gift bag

No-Guilt Trail Mix

1 quart air-popped corn or corn popped with no
    more than 1 teaspoon canola oil
Butter-flavored cooking spray or reconstituted
    butter-flavored granules
1 tablespoon dried Mexican seasoning
⅓ cup dried cranberries, blueberries, or cherries
1 tablespoon dry roasted pumpkin seeds

Put popcorn in a large bowl and lightly spray with cooking spray. Sprinkle with Mexican seasoning. Spray and toss again. Add remaining ingredients. Eat within a few hours.

MAKES 1 SERVING

337 calories, 5 grams fat, 86 milligrams sodium

(377 calories, 10 grams fat, 86 milligrams sodium if popped with 1 teaspoon canola oil)

ONION POPCORN

1 quart air-popped corn or corn popped with
   no more than 1 teaspoon canola oil
Butter-flavored cooking spray or reconstituted
   butter-flavored granules
2 tablespoons dried onion soup and recipe mix
$\frac{1}{2}$ teaspoon garlic powder
$\frac{1}{8}$ teaspoon cayenne pepper

Put popcorn in a large bowl and lightly spray with cooking spray. In a small bowl, combine remaining ingredients. Sprinkle over popcorn and toss to coat evenly. Spray and toss again. Serve at once.

MAKES 1 SERVING

146 calories, trace fat, trace sodium

(186 calories, 5 grams fat, trace sodium if popped with 1 teaspoon canola oil)

ORANGE POPCORN

1 quart air-popped corn or corn popped with no
    more than 1 teaspoon canola oil
Butter-flavored cooking spray or reconstituted
    butter-flavored granules
3 tablespoons orange-flavored powder drink mix,
    already sweetened with sugar substitute
½ teaspoon dried orange peel

Put popcorn in a large bowl and lightly spray with cooking spray. Sprinkle with orange drink mix and dried orange peel; toss to coat evenly. Spray and toss again. Serve at once.

MAKES 1 SERVING

204 calories, trace fat, 13 milligrams sodium

(244 calories, 5 grams fat, 13 milligrams sodium if popped with 1 teaspoon of canola oil)

POPCORN AND APPLE PIE

1 quart air-popped corn or corn popped with
    no more than 1 teaspoon canola oil
Butter-flavored cooking spray or reconstituted
    butter-flavored granules
1 ½ teaspoons ground cinnamon
½ teaspoon ground nutmeg
¼ teaspoon ground cloves
1 tablespoon granulated sugar substitute
½ cup dried apples

Put popcorn in a large bowl and lightly spray with cooking spray. In a small bowl, combine cinnamon, nutmeg, cloves, and sugar substitute. Sprinkle over popcorn; toss to coat evenly. Spray and toss again. Stir in apples and serve at once.

MAKES 1 SERVING

225 calories, < 1 gram fat, 40 milligrams sodium

(265 calories, 5 grams fat, 40 milligrams sodium if popped with 1 teaspoon canola oil)

Popcorn: A Natural Packing Material

Protect fragile gifts for shipping or mailing by surrounding with popped corn. Air-popped corn, made without oil, is preferred, but unless the package is going to sit for several months before opening, you can also use popcorn that has been popped in oil. The popcorn offers better protection than excelsior, and popcorn is recyclable. The popcorn can be eaten or thrown out for the birds—they love popcorn, too!

Popcorn Croutons

Scatter a handful of popped corn over a piping hot bowl of soup for extra flavor, color, and texture. A great way to use leftover popcorn!

POPCORN PROVENÇAL

1 quart air-popped corn or corn popped with
    no more than 1 teaspoon canola oil
Butter-flavored cooking spray or reconstituted
    butter-flavored granules
1 teaspoon mixed dried Italian herbs
$\frac{1}{8}$ teaspoon garlic powder
$\frac{1}{8}$ teaspoon paprika

Put popcorn in a large bowl and lightly spray with cooking spray. Sprinkle with remaining ingredients; toss to coat evenly. Spray and toss again. Serve at once.

MAKES 1 SERVING

107 calories, trace fat, < 1 milligram sodium

(147 calories, 5 grams fat, < 1 milligram sodium if popped with 1 teaspoon canola oil)

POPCORN WITH A KICK

1 quart air-popped corn or corn popped with
no more than 1 teaspoon canola oil
Butter-flavored cooking spray or reconstituted
butter-flavored granules
1 teaspoon wasabi powder
½ teaspoon garlic powder

Put popcorn in a large bowl and lightly spray with cooking spray. Sprinkle with wasabi powder and garlic powder; toss to coat evenly. Spray and toss again. Serve at once.

MAKES 1 SERVING

111 calories, trace fat, 165 milligrams sodium

(151 calories, 5 grams fat, 165 milligrams sodium if popped with 1 teaspoon canola oil)

Scandinavian Dill Popcorn

1 quart air-popped corn or corn popped with
  no more than 1 teaspoon canola oil
Butter-flavored cooking spray or reconstituted
  butter-flavored granules
2 tablespoons dried ranch-style dip mix
1 teaspoon dill weed
½ teaspoon onion powder
¼ teaspoon dried lemon peel

Put popcorn in a large bowl and lightly spray with cooking spray. Sprinkle with remaining ingredients. Toss to coat evenly. Spray and toss again. Serve at once.

MAKES 1 SERVING

109 calories, trace fat, 38 milligrams sodium

(149 calories, 5 grams fat, 38 milligrams sodium if popped with 1 teaspoon canola oil)

Popcorn in the Movies

Popcorn has been a part of the movie experience on both sides of the screen. In *Camp Nowhere*, a 1994 comedy starring Christopher Lloyd, kids who are running their own summer camp make a "dee-licious" popcorn omelet.

In the final scene of the 1985 satire *Real Genius,* starring Val Kilmer and William Atherton, the whiz-kids direct a laser beam designed for assassinations from outer space onto a 20-foot-wide expandable package of popcorn kernels. As the popcorn pops, it fills the house and appears to physically lift the roof off the house. As credits roll, the children of the town are playing and "swimming" in the yard full of popcorn.

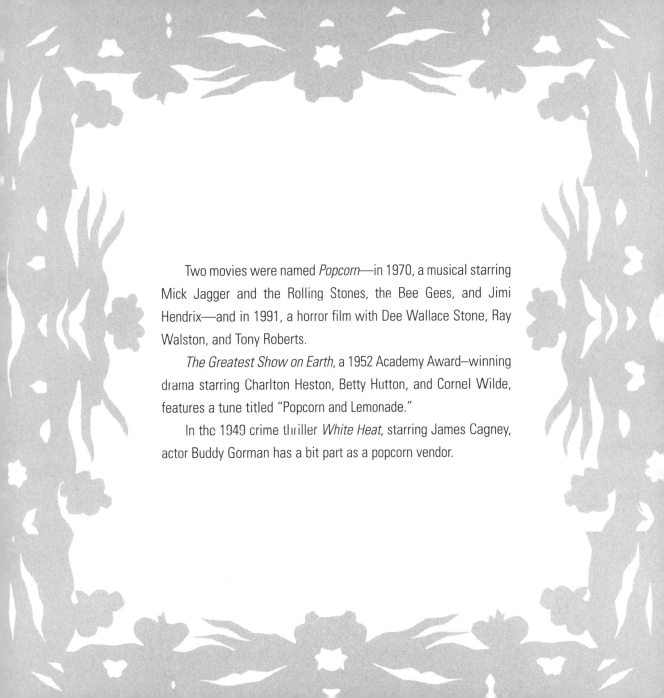

Two movies were named *Popcorn*—in 1970, a musical starring Mick Jagger and the Rolling Stones, the Bee Gees, and Jimi Hendrix—and in 1991, a horror film with Dee Wallace Stone, Ray Walston, and Tony Roberts.

The Greatest Show on Earth, a 1952 Academy Award–winning drama starring Charlton Heston, Betty Hutton, and Cornel Wilde, features a tune titled "Popcorn and Lemonade."

In the 1949 crime thriller *White Heat*, starring James Cagney, actor Buddy Gorman has a bit part as a popcorn vendor.

Sweet 'n' Spicy Popcorn

1 quart air-popped corn or corn popped with
no more than 1 teaspoon canola oil
Butter-flavored cooking spray or reconstituted
butter-flavored granules
3 tablespoons granulated sugar substitute
½ teaspoon ground cinnamon
¼ teaspoon ground nutmeg
½ teaspoon dried orange peel

Preheat oven to 300° F. Spread popcorn on a nonstick cookie sheet and lightly spray with cooking spray. In a small bowl, combine remaining ingredients. Sprinkle over popcorn and toss to coat evenly. Spray and toss again. Bake for 10 minutes, tossing once. Serve warm.

MAKES 1 SERVING

118 calories, trace fat, trace sodium

(158 calories, 5 grams fat, trace sodium if popped with 1 teaspoon oil)

Popcorn Sales
for Charity

In 1984, Paul Newman, a great film actor and philanthropist, added popcorn to his growing list of food items sold through Newman's Own food company, which awards 100 percent of its after-tax profits to charities. For 1993 alone, the amount came to nearly $7 million in grants, approximately one-third of which was derived from the sale of popcorn.

Wyandot Popcorn Museum

Located in Heritage Hall in Marion, Ohio, just 45 miles north of Columbus, the Wyandot Popcorn Museum houses the world's largest collection of restored antique popcorn poppers and peanut roasters, many dating back to the 19th and early 20th centuries. For museum hours and information, call (614) 387-4255.

3-Alarm Popcorn

1 quart air-popped corn or corn popped with
no more than 1 teaspoon canola oil
Butter-flavored cooking spray or reconstituted
butter-flavored granules
1/4 teaspoon ground ginger
1/4 teaspoon ground mustard
1/4 teaspoon onion powder
1/8 teaspoon allspice
1/8 teaspoon garlic powder
1/8 teaspoon paprika
1/8 teaspoon crushed dried thyme
1/8 teaspoon dried lemon peel
Dash cayenne pepper

Put popcorn in a large bowl and lightly spray with cooking spray. In a small bowl, combine remaining ingredients. Sprinkle over popcorn; toss to coat evenly. Spray and toss again. Serve at once.

MAKES 1 SERVING

111 calories, trace fat, 1 milligram sodium

(151 calories, 5 grams fat, 1 milligram sodium if popped with 1 teaspoon oil)

Acknowledgments

Many thanks for historical and other pertinent information on popcorn to the Popcorn Institute, Chicago, Illinois; Strawberry Banke Museum, Portsmouth, New Hampshire; Wyandot Popcorn Museum, Marion, Ohio; the National Dairy Board, Arlington, Virginia; Sears Merchandise Group, Hoffman Estates, Illinois; Newman's Own, Westport, Connecticut; American Pop Corn Company, Sioux City, Iowa; and Plimouth Plantation, Plymouth, Massachusetts.

About the Author

Frances Towner Giedt is a home economist who holds a double degree in foods and nutrition and journalism. She is a consultant to restaurants and food manufacturers and is co-author of *The Joslin Diabetes Gourmet Cookbook: Heart-Healthy Recipes for Family and Friends* (Bantam Books) and culinary author of *Kitchen Herbs* (Bantam Books). Her most recent book is *Something Spicy* (Simon & Schuster). She has homes in Wilton, Connecticut, and Fort Worth, Texas, where several popcorn poppers occupy a special place in her kitchens—and heart.